# CONTENTS

C000179631

# WALK BIRMINGHAM

The 20 walks in this book will take you on a journey through time. You will see evidence of Birmingham's long and fascinating history, from Bronze Age burnt mounds to medieval churches, moated manors and industrial heritage. The walks are circular, varying in length from under a mile to just over three miles. They explore areas all over the city from Sutton Coldfield to Longbridge and Harborne to Sheldon.

All the start points can be reached by public transport. Many have great cafes near the start/finish, several in one of Birmingham Museums' historic properties. See our website www.birminghammuseums.org.uk for opening times and more information.

Paths can be muddy in wet weather, so plan ahead and wear sensible footwear. Be aware of road traffic and take sensible precautions en route. We hope you enjoy walking yourself healthy while you explore the city's past.

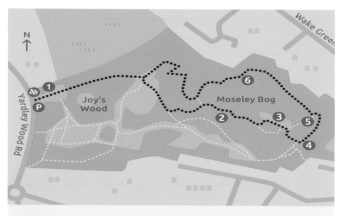

 ## MOSELEY BOG

*Using a wet valley*

 Start/Finish: **Entrance to Moseley Bog, off Yardley Wood Road.**
Postcode: **B13 9JX.**

 Bus service: **From City Centre stop on Yardley Wood Road.**

 Parking: **Small car park, B13 9JX.**

 Facilities: **Café at Sarehole Mill.**

 Length: **1.25 km / 0.78 miles.**
On boardwalks and unsurfaced paths with some steps. May be
muddy in wet weather. Boggy ground and open water in places.

 Dog-friendly.

 Time: **30 minutes.**  Step count: **2,200 steps.**

**START**

JRR Tolkien lived near Moseley Bog as a boy and the place inspired his descriptions of ancient forests in his books *The Lord of the Rings and The Hobbit*.

**1** At the car park take the path to the left of the information panel. When you come to a field on the right, cross the grass to go into the woods then continue along a path. When you reach a viewpoint take a flight of steps down into the valley.

Turn left at the bottom, then when you reach the boardwalk across a stream turn right. Soon you come to an interpretation panel. The raised ground in front of you, on both sides of the stream is a burnt mound, radiocarbon dated to the Bronze Age, about 1000 B.C. Burnt mounds are piles of heat-shattered stones and charcoal, often near streams, which have been found in many parts of the British Isles. Other than a few finds of tools and weapons they are the only tangible evidence of people living in Birmingham during the Bronze Age because their houses and

BURNT MOUND

fields now lie under modern development. Burnt mounds were used either for cooking, using the heated stones to boil water, or to create steam for sauna-type bathing. The mounds excavated in Birmingham contained no tools or animal bones so they are more likely to be the remains of Bronze Age saunas.

**2** Continue along the boardwalk a little further until the stream straightens out and the ground is flatter, just before a fork in the path. This is where the sweat lodge would have been. Excavations on other burnt mounds have revealed holes left by thin branches. These were driven into the ground and bent over to form the frame of a tent-like structure which could be covered in animal skins. Inside it was space for several people to sit around a hollow containing stones heated on the nearby fire while water taken from the stream was poured onto the stones to create steam. Several experimental reconstructions of sweat lodges have been undertaken at Moseley Bog to test this interpretation.

**3** Take the left fork in the path and you come to a platform overlooking an area of wetland full of rushes. This is what much of the area of Moseley Bog looked like in the Bronze Age. It was probably regarded as a magical place, and sweat lodges may have had religious significance or have been associated with important social occasions throughout the year. Continue on the boardwalk turning first to the left and then to the right at the junction.

**4** Carry on until you reach a bridge to your right over the stream and a flight of sleeper steps going up a broad high bank of ground ahead of you and to the left. This bank is the dam of a 17th- or 18th-century pond which filled most of what is now Moseley Bog and was a feeder for the millpond that powered Sarehole Mill. Brickwork in the gap where the stream cuts through the dam is the remains of a sluice system to control the water level in the pond. Take the steps to the left up onto the top of the dam and follow a narrow sleeper path along the

STEPS UP TO DAM

top until you come to a pond. This pond is in the base of a large hollow formed when material was extracted to build the dam. It later became a garden pond. Note how the end of the dam curves around away to the left, giving it extra strength.

DAM

REMAINS OF VICTORIAN GLASSHOUSES

**5** Turn left at the end of the dam and walk up a rough narrow path bearing right (stay on the main path) until you reach the brick foundations of a group of former glasshouses and outbuildings. These were once in the gardens of Victorian houses built on high ground to your right, where there is now a modern school.

WOODLAND VIEW

**6** Continue on the path constructed of tree branches and brick paving (this can be muddy!), then along another narrow sleeper path which zig-zags through boggy ground. Upon reaching a junction with another boardwalk turn right, then continue up the slope until you come to another information panel and a red shale path going to the left along the edge of an open field. This will bring you back to the car park.

FINISH

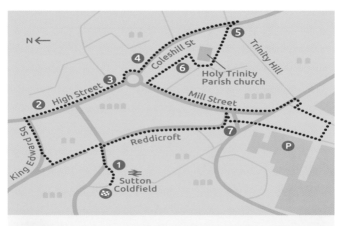

# SUTTON COLDFIELD CENTRE

## *From the railway to the medieval town*

 Start/Finish: Sutton Coldfield Station, Railway Road. Postcode: B73 6AY.

Bus service: From City Centre stop in The Parade approx. 350m.

**P** Parking: Various car parks in town centre.

Facilities: Places to eat in Gracechurch Centre.

Length: 1.4 km / 0.87 miles.
On pavements and paths. Some steps.

Dog-friendly.

Time: 30 minutes.     Step count: 2,800 steps.

**START**

Standing outside Sutton Coldfield Station and looking straight ahead, the building you see to the left of the modern building was originally a hotel. It was built in 1863, overlooking what was then the railway terminus, and later became the Council House.

**1** Turn right up Railway Road then left up an alley opposite Reddicroft into King Edward's Square. On your left the former Council House and Town Hall (with clock tower) are a reminder that Sutton Coldfield was a separate local authority, from the creation of its first governing body in 1528 until its absorption by Birmingham in 1974. Cross King Edward's Square, past the war memorial and follow the road downhill to High Street.

**2** When you arrive on High Street, take a look around. High Street runs north towards Lichfield and Tamworth. Sutton Park originally extended right up to it. Buildings were first constructed along the road, and the park reduced in size, as part of the development of the town by the Earls of Warwick in the 13th century. More buildings were added in

THE THREE TUNS, HIGH STREET

13

the 16th century and subsequently. Some buildings, such as the Royal Hotel to your left, were built in the 18th century, but in some cases brick frontages were added to older buildings of this time. Walk along High Street to your right, past the Three Tuns with its former cart entrance archway, and look across the road. The modern buildings, numbers 32 and 34, are both on the sites of stone buildings which dated to the 16th century. Continue along the road towards the church. Vesey House, over the road to your right, was built in 1635 for the then Rector. It was the first brick building in the High Street.

**3** Cross Midland Drive, named after the Midland Railway Company which built a railway line under the town centre and across Sutton Park. At the next junction look across the road island to the stone gable wall of the brick building opposite. This was built in stone in 1623 after an earlier timber-framed building had burned down. The brickwork on the front is 18th-century in date. In front of you is Mill Street, which runs across the valley of the Ebrook towards Birmingham. You are standing at its junction with High Street to your right and Coleshill Street, which

HOLY TRINITY CHURCH

14

led to Warwick and eventually to London, on your left. This road junction was a market place - a charter was granted for a weekly market in 1300 - and the site of the 16th-century Moot Hall, the meeting place of the town's governing body, which had a covered market place and dungeon under it.

**4** Continue along Coleshill Street and look through the archway (white gates) on the left where you can see the stone wall of another older building that was later given a brick frontage. Further along, on the other side of the road you can see the oldest part of Holy Trinity church. The stepped plinth at the base of the wall dates to the 13th century. Continue to the junction with Rectory Road, where excavations revealed a medieval oven and a flint axe that was about 50,000 years old. Cross over Rectory Road and then over Coleshill Street at the crossing. Detailed examination of buildings here has shown that some of them have medieval origins.

**5** Cross over Trinity Hill and take the steps into the churchyard. There was a priest in Sutton in about 1200 and the oldest parts of the church are 13th-century, but it was rebuilt and extended in the 16th, 18th and 19th centuries. Continue around the church and past the 15th-century tower. Just past the church turn right up the steps into the churchyard and head for a wrought-iron gateway into Vesey Gardens where you get a fine view along the High Street and down Coleshill Street. Go down the steps and looking back you will see a plaque about Bishop Vesey, a native of Sutton Coldfield and a great benefactor of the town.

**6** Take the path through the gardens to the road junction and turn left down Mill Street. Excavations on the other side of the road, before new development, revealed remains of medieval timber buildings and stone footings of buildings like those in the High Street. A medieval watermill stood at the bottom of the hill on the site now occupied by McDonalds. Cross over Victoria Road at the crossing and walk into Lower Parade. The mill was powered by water from a large pool and you are now are walking along the dam that created it. The high slope in front of the shops opposite is the Parade, built in the 19th century to improve the route across the valley. You can see the slope of the dam in the gap between the buildings on your left, near the bus stops. Cross at the crossing and turn right along the front of the shopping centre. The mill pool occupied all the area of the shopping centre and extended back towards Sutton Park.

GATEWAY TO VESEY GARDENS AND BUILDINGS IN COLESHILL STREET BEYOND

**7** Cross the road opposite the Gate Inn, then turn left around the pub and go up the hill. Look through the driveway just past the modern buildings to see the 17th-century brickwork of Vesey House. Continue along Reddicroft then onto Railway Road to get back to the station.

FINISH

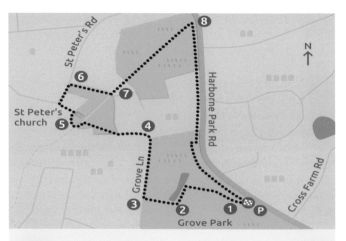

# HARBORNE

*A rural landscape*

 Start/Finish: **Harborne Park Road.** Postcode: **B17 0BL.**

 Bus service: From City Centre stop on High Street.

 Parking: Car park for Grove Park on Harborne Park Road.

 Facilities: The Bell public house and many places on Harborne High Street 1km.

 Length: 1.8 km / 1.12 miles.
On pavement, surfaced paths and mown grass paths.
Open water near pool in park.

 Dog-friendly.

 Time: 45 minutes.     Step count: 3,000 steps.

Before its suburban growth in the 19th century, Harborne consisted of scattered houses, with clusters along the present High Street and around St Peter's church.

**1** From the car park go through the gate in the white wrought-iron fence. This estate fencing dates back to Victorian times. Look out for places where the tree trunks have actually grown around the fencing! Walk downhill along a mown grass path towards the pool, heading for the trunk of a cut tree on raised ground. You are walking over ridges, the remains of cultivation in the medieval period. When you reach the pool turn left along the path. This pool was probably originally constructed as a fishpond in the Middle Ages but was formalised to become part of the parkland setting for the 18th-century house known as the Grove.

**2** Continue to the end of the pool and take the path up towards a level area of tarmac. You have been walking through the former grounds of the Grove and are now standing on the site of the house

GROVE PARK

itself. It was originally built as a farmhouse which was extended in the 18th century. It was the home of Thomas Atwood, who was one of Birmingham's first two MPs, serving from 1832-9. Atwood founded the Birmingham Political Union 'of the Lower and Middle Classes of the People' and played an instrumental role nationally in the electoral reform movement. Look out for a plaque set into the ground commemorating the fact that he lived here between 1783 and 1856. After he died the house was rebuilt in 1877–8, by architect John Henry Chamberlain for William Kenrick, a prominent Birmingham businessman and MP for Birmingham North. Kenrick died at the Grove, aged 88, in 1919. This house was demolished in 1963 but a fine panelled ante-room was saved and is now on display in the Victoria and Albert Museum in London. All you can see now are the steps which led down from the house to its gardens. The large cedar tree to your left looking towards the road is said to have been planted in about 1785 by Thomas Green.

**3** Walk across the small car park to Grove Lane and turn right. The gate piers on the corner at the junction with Old Church Road are the entrance to Harborne Hall (private, no public access), which was originally built in the 18th century by Thomas Green, a wealthy ironmaster who lived nearby, for his daughter. It is likely that this was the site of an earlier manor house. The present house is 19th-century in date. Through the gate on the other side of the road you can get a glimpse of Bishops Croft (private, no public access), originally Harborne House, built in the 18th century for Thomas Green.

**4** Turn left along Old Church Road and enter the churchyard through the lych gate. Take the path to your left. Walk around the outside of the church and before going under the archway ahead of you, stop and look at the church. Most of it was rebuilt in the 19th century but as you pass through the archway you can see the tower - which dates to the 14th and 15th centuries. On the side nearest to you there is a 14th-century window, and as you walk around the tower you can

see a 15th-century window above the entrance and a 14th-century niche or recess on the far side. The worn stones at the base may be the plinth of an even older tower. The church is thought to have its origins as a minster church in Anglo-Saxon times, serving a very large parish which included Smethwick, Edgbaston, West Bromwich, Handsworth and central Birmingham.

TOWER AND ARCHWAY OF ST PETER'S CHURCH

**5** Walk down the footpath opposite the tower to Old Church Road. Over the road you can see Elmley Lodge, a grand 19th-century house, and to your right the Bell Inn built on the site of a 16th-century farmhouse. The present building was constructed from the 17th-century onwards. There are 19th-century semi-detached houses next to it. Bear right around the edge of the churchyard; notice the white cottage at the junction with St Peters Road which dates to the 1830s.

**6** Keep the churchyard wall to your right, and just past the school (opposite another lych gate) you get another glimpse of Bishops Croft through a gate. The chapel on this site was built in 1923 after the house was acquired by the Diocese of Birmingham. Looking back across the school playground, the small brick building with a chimney on each end was built as the master's house in 1837, and around it are other

THE BELL INN

school buildings added during the 19th century.

**7** Turn left down the footpath, Old Church Avenue. When you come to the cricket pitches, you can see the front of Bishops Croft once more to the right. Low ridges in the grass to your left are remains of former cultivation in Riddings or Weddings Field, one of the medieval open fields of Harborne. Each person in the community was allotted strips of land to farm. The strips were scattered across the field to ensure that everyone had a share of good and poor land, and the ridges correspond to those strips.

**8** At the end of the footpath turn right along Harborne Park Road. Continue along this road until you eventually come to the entrance to the Park next to an entrance lodge, alongside what was once the drive leading to the front of the Grove. From here you will see the pool to your right and the white wrought-iron railings you looked at earlier are ahead of you. Head for this, walking through the park back to the car park.

FINISH

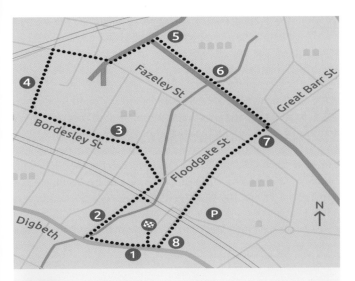

 **DIGBETH**

*From Bird's Custard and Typhoo Tea to river Rea*

 Start/Finish: The Custard Factory, Gibb Street. Postcode: B9 4AA.

 Bus service: From City Centre stop on High Street, Deritend.

 Parking: Trinity Street, B9 4AG.

 Facilities: The Custard Factory.

 Length: 2 km / 1.24 miles.
On pavements and canal towpaths.

 Dog-friendly.

 Time: 45 minutes.  Step count: 3,200 steps.

**START**

The Custard Factory originated as Alfred Bird's Devonshire Works in 1866, producing the well-known powdered custard. Mrs Bird was allergic to eggs, so her husband invented this egg-free alternative to traditional egg custard.

**1** Walk along the main road towards the city centre, passing the front of the Devonshire Works. Where the road rises slightly, you are crossing the River Rea. This small river was not where Birmingham began, but its water powered mills and it was used in industries such as leather tanning. Turn right into Floodgate Street at the J F Kennedy Memorial. Once you have passed it, look back at the South and City Birmingham College. The oldest part was built as a Board School in 1891. Excavations on the site of the new buildings revealed remains of leather tanning from the 16th century onwards. Floodgate Street is named after the floodgates that let water from the river Rea into a side channel which bypassed Heath Mill further down the river.

**2** Walk towards the viaduct you can see ahead of you. This carried the Great Western Railway line over the Rea valley to Snow Hill Station, which was opened in 1852. Under the viaduct the entrance to your right (usually open in daytime) takes you into massive spaces beneath the railway line, decorated with street art. It leads to a footbridge over the river Rea, which flows along a brick culvert built in 1893. After exploring this area return to Floodgate Street

CUSTARD FACTORY, DEVONSHIRE WORKS

BENEATH BORDESLEY VIADUCT / RIVER REA

and just before turning left into Little Ann Street look ahead towards an attractive Victorian building with a curved frontage on the corner with River Street, which was built as a medical mission in 1880.

**3** Continue along Little Ann Street and at the road junction cross over into Bordesley Street. This road was originally a lane running across fields behind the medieval town, which was centred on St Martin's church and the Bullring. The grid-like pattern of streets on either side was laid out in the 18th and 19th centuries. On the right, opposite the junction with Oxford Street, are the former Typhoo Tea Company's premises, built in 1931. At the next junction, on the corner with Meriden Street, the former Spotted Dog is one of several corner public houses in the area. Built about 1810, it is now decorated with street art.

**4** Turn right along New Canal Street then right into Fazeley Street. From the road bridge over the canal you can see Typhoo Wharf to your right. Over the road the blue brick buildings were constructed in 1850 as offices for the Grand Junction Canal Company, with warehouses

GUN BARREL PROOF HOUSE

behind them. Take the path from Fazeley Street down to the canal. You are now on the Digbeth Branch Canal, completed in 1790, running from the Birmingham and Fazeley Canal near Dartmouth Circus. Continue along the towpath and over the canal bridge. From the bridge you can see the Gun Barrel Proof House, built in 1813 to improve the quality of guns made in Birmingham. It is still in use for testing firearms today.

**5** After crossing the bridge turn immediately left, walking back beneath the bridge you just crossed, onto the towpath of the Grand Union (Warwick) Canal, which was opened in 1799. Note the grooves cut on the bridge by towropes. On the other side of the canal is a stop lock, designed to control the flow between the different canal companies' water, and a covered dock and warehouse. Behind these Warwick Wharf was entered by two canal basins, both now filled in. One was at the end of the stop lock, and the position of the other is indicated by the curving wall of the Fellows, Morton and Clayton building.

STOP LOCK

**6** Continue along the towpath and cross the viaduct over the river Rea. Just after this you will see a roofless building with a painting of a fox on the end wall on the other side of canal. This is the retort house of the Fazeley Street gasworks (1837), in which gas was made by heating coal. The coal used as both fuel and raw material was brought along the canal. The next building, the Bond, was a warehouse with an adjoining canal basin, built in 1884.

Carry on along the towpath, crossing a bridge that once passed over a canal arm, then walk under a railway bridge. Just past the next road bridge immediately ahead of you, leave the towpath via the path on your left. Turn left along Great Barr Street, crossing over the canal you just walked alongside. Across the road you can see a railway viaduct that ends abruptly. This was built towards Curzon Street in 1848 by the Great Western Railway, but was never completed because the rival London and North Western railway company refused to release land.

**7** At the next road junction, note the 19ᵗʰ-century cast iron urinal on the left (a listed building!) and the white building diagonally opposite, now Fazeley Studios, a former chapel and Sunday school (1865/ 1876).

Keep walking straight down Heath Mill Lane, named after a medieval corn mill which stood on the other side of Fazeley Street. On the left is the distinctive St Basil's church, built in a Romanesque style in 1910-11. Digbeth was once covered with densely packed `back to back' and courtyard housing, and the population needed churches, schools and the library which you can see at the end of the road, on your right.

**8** Shortly after passing beneath the railway viaduct you come to the junction with High Street. The timber-framed Old Crown on the left was built in the 15th century (not 1368 as its sign says), as a guildhall and school. Excavations have shown that pottery was being made on the site in the 13th century, and metalworking and leather tanning took place nearby.

Turn to the right and you arrive back at The Custard Factory.

FINISH

THE OLD CROWN

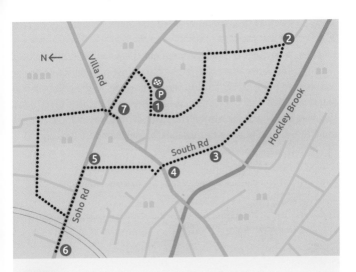

 ## AROUND SOHO HOUSE

*From Matthew Boulton's Manufactory to Soho Road*

 Start/Finish: **Soho House Museum. Postcode: B18 5LB.**

Bus service: **From City Centre stop on Soho Hill.**

Parking: **Soho House Museum or street parking.**

Facilities: **Café at Soho House Museum.**

Length: **2 km / 1.24 miles.**
**On pavements.**

Dog-friendly.

Time: **45 minutes.**　　　　Step count: **3,200 steps.**

START

Matthew Boulton established the Soho Manufactory in 1761 on the site of an existing watermill on the Hockley Brook. A wide range of products was made here and Boulton employed innovative processes. James Watt's first working steam engine was used to pump water back to the water wheel in the polishing mill, and it was the site of the first steam-powered mint in the world. The last surviving building of the Manufactory was demolished in 1863. Find out more by visiting Soho House Museum (birminghammuseums.org.uk)

SOHO HOUSE

**1** At the entrance to Soho House turn left along Soho Avenue, then left along Vicarage Road and right at the junction with Park Avenue. Soho House was built for Matthew Boulton on the site of an earlier cottage, in the mid 18th century, when this area was open countryside. It was not unusual at the time for an industrialist to want to live close to his factory, but Boulton also created extensive pleasure grounds around his new house and was a keen gardener. After his death there were attempts to preserve part of the estate as a public park, but it was eventually sold off in lots for development, along with the site of his manufactory. Park Avenue was one of the roads laid out at a time when remnants of the parkland survived. Several large villa-style houses were built here in the mid 19th century, some of which you can still see today. Continue right down Park Avenue and notice the steep slope taking you into the valley of the Hockley Brook.

**2** Turn right into South Road. The buildings of the Soho Manufactory lay on both sides of this road. Opposite the junction with South Road Avenue, is the site of the mint and buildings where latchets were made (removable shoe buckles). The site is under the houses and their gardens on your right (no remains are visible and it is private land). The original buildings were later replaced by a steam-powered cutting-room for coin blanks. Excavations by television's Time Team in the gardens behind these houses revealed remains of buildings and a brick tunnel which originally contained the drive shaft of a steam engine.

**3** Keep walking along South Road. On the left side of this road the Principal Building of the Manufactory extended roughly from the entrance to a yard just past South Road Avenue as far as St Michaels Road, and down the slope to the left to Hockley Brook, which runs through the present industrial area beyond. This was a massive industrial building for its time, containing workshops, showrooms, warehouses and living accommodation. The original intention had been to operate machinery using water power from the brook. When it became apparent that there was insufficient water to meet the needs of the manufactory Boulton entered into partnership with James Watt to develop his steam engine technology. This was to revolutionise industrial processes across the globe, and meant that factories were no longer tied to sites near rivers for the generation of power to drive machinery.

**4** Continue to St Michael's Hill and cross over to read the interpretation panel at the end of Scholars Close, looking back towards the site of the Manufactory. Next, walk along Scholars Close for a

LANSDOWNE TERRACE

short distance and take the footpath on the right, at the end of the school boundary fence. This leads into Piers Road, then turn left onto Soho Road. When the Manufactory was first built, much of this area was heathland which extended across Hockley Brook into Birmingham. The main road across it, now Soho Hill and Soho Road, was developed as a turnpike road in 1727 and buildings were constructed along it in the late 18th century and early 19th century. At the junction of Piers Road and Soho Road is a good example of these buildings; the white building to your right, Lansdowne Terrace, was constructed in about 1840. By this time Handsworth had become a fashionable upper-middle class suburb on the rural fringes of the industrial towns of Birmingham and the Black Country.

**5** Cross at the crossing and go left along Soho Road. Just after Ivy Road you will cross over the railway line. At the junction with Belgrave Terrace are the Rhodes Almshouses, built in 1873 on land given by Matilda Rhodes for 15 almshouses for poor, aged women of

RHODES ALMSHOUSES

Birmingham, and a matron's house. The clock tower in the distance is that of the former Council House of Handsworth Urban District Council built, with the adjoining library, in 1878-9.

**6** Retrace your steps back along Soho Road then turn left up Ivy Road. Cross over Whitehall Road and continue to the junction with Rose Hill Road. Ahead of you, you can see King Edward VI Grammar School for Girls which was designed by Philip Chatwin and opened in 1911. Continue to the right along Rose Hill Road past the Methodist church on the left and the Nishkam Centre on your right.

**7** Cross Soho Road at the crossing and go down St Michaels Road to St Michael's church. Matthew Boulton would have attended St Mary's church (see Handsworth Park walk), where he is buried. St Michael's church was built in 1855, when the Manufactory had gone out of use and its buildings were being demolished, to serve people living along Soho Road and in the houses built on Boulton's estate. Return to Soho Road and turn right past more grand 19th-century houses with elaborate doorways and bay windows. The house at the corner with Soho Avenue has Corinthian-style (acanthus plant) decoration. The archway on its right led to the stables, which were in the building with arches behind the house. You can see this from Soho Avenue, on your right hand side. Take this road and Soho House is a short distance away on your left.

FINISH

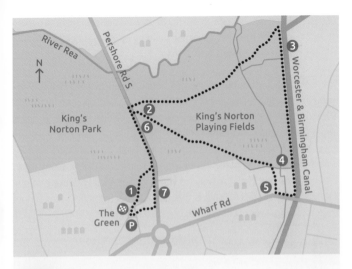

# KING'S NORTON

*From a medieval village to a canal*

Start/Finish: **The Green.** Postcode: **B38 8RU.**

Bus service: **From City Centre stop on Pershore Road South.**

Parking: **The Green.**

Facilities: **Café at St Nicholas Place.**

Length: **2.2km / 1.37 miles.**
**On pavements, gravel paths and open water along canal.
Some steps.**

Dog-friendly.

Time: **45 minutes.**          Step count: **3,400 steps.**

START

From The Green walk north towards the church, stopping outside the timber-framed building on the left before entering the churchyard.

St Nicolas Place (the former Saracen's Head) is a fine medieval timber-framed building. Tree-ring dating showed that it was constructed in the 15th century. Archaeological excavations revealed even older remains under the building, including timber buildings of 13th- and 14th-century date. Some decorated tiles forming the floor of the 15th century building were still in place - they were the medieval equivalent of an expensive carpet. The discovery of some Roman pottery dating to the 1st and 2nd centuries AD shows that people were living here long before these buildings were constructed.

**1** Enter the churchyard through the lych gate, near which you will find an interpretation panel, and take the path to the right of the church. Walk to the far end of the church and look back at it.

The oldest part of St Nicolas church is the chancel, where you can see a small round-headed 12th-century window. The church was originally a chapel belonging to Bromsgrove church. It was substantially extended in the 13th and 14th centuries and the tower, spire and porch

ST NICOLAS CHURCH AND THE SARACEN'S HEAD

THE OLD GRAMMAR SCHOOL

were added in the 15th century.

Continue along the churchyard path to the Old Grammar School. It was constructed in the 17th century on a newly-built brick ground floor, re-using materials from a 15th-century timber-framed building that originally stood on another site in King's Norton.

After looking at the Grammar School, take the path down to the right. Exit the churchyard through a metal gate and turn left onto the main road, Pershore Road South. You will pass the formal civic gardens on your left, originally laid out in the 1920s and recently restored, before crossing at the traffic lights.

**2** Take the surfaced path straight ahead through King's Norton playing fields. Cross a bridge over a stream that was originally called the Lint or Leontan Brook, mentioned in a charter of about AD

700 as one of the boundaries of an area of woodland called Hellerelege, to the east of King's Norton village. After the bridge you soon reach the Worcester and Birmingham Canal. This starts at Gas Street Basin in the city centre and had been built this far by 1796, joining the Stratford on Avon Canal in front of you. It was gradually extended and eventually reached Worcester by 1815.

**3** Turn along the footpath to your right. The building you pass immediately on your right was a toll house built in 1796 to control traffic at the junction of the two canals. Continue along the towpath.

**4** Walk past some new houses on your right, and leave the canal just before the bridge, taking the path up to Wharf Road. From the bridge, look to your left, up Parsons Hill. Remains of Roman buildings dating from the 1st to the 3rd centuries AD were found near here, consisting of the remains of timber-framed buildings together with

CANAL JUNCTION

CANAL FEEDER AT KING'S NORTON PLAYING FIELDS

pebble surfaces that may have been part of the Roman Ryknield Street. Turn right along Wharf Road and right again just before the Baptist church (built in 1815) to enter the playing fields. You will soon cross a bridge. You are crossing the canal feeder which runs from Wychall Reservoir, built in about 1821 to ensure water levels were maintained in the canal.

**5** Turn left following the gravel path running alongside the canal feeder and just before you reach a car park, in the field on your left (with a view of the church spire), you can see remains of ridge and furrow, the results of medieval cultivation.

**6** Continue through the car park, out of the playing fields. Turning left uphill along the main road you will pass a series of municipal buildings. These include King's Norton Library, built in 1905 and part-funded by philanthropist Andrew Carnegie, and a fine set of red terracotta school buildings and master's house, built in 1878 and extended in 1912. Cross at the traffic lights, bear left, and take the ramp through a car park back up to The Green.

**7** Take a look around for some other remains of medieval King's Norton. Number 3 is built on the site of a timber-framed building which had jettied gables like those on the Saracen's Head, but its final fragments were demolished in 1982. The timber-framed left-hand gable of number 10, the Select & Save supermarket, is one wing of a 15th-century building which originally had a great hall to the right. Further on, near the corner, excavations before the construction of James Court revealed remains of 13th- and 14th-century timber buildings. Archaeologists discovered that people who lived here used pottery made in the Bullring area, and in north Worcestershire, north Warwickshire and Buckinghamshire.

This site may have been abandoned by the end of the 14th century, possibly as a result of economic decline following the Black Death. The construction of the Saracen's Head and other large timber-framed buildings and the addition of the tower, spire and porch to St Nicolas church demonstrate the subsequent spectacular revival of King's Norton in the 15th century. Once you've had a look around, return to The Green.

FINISH

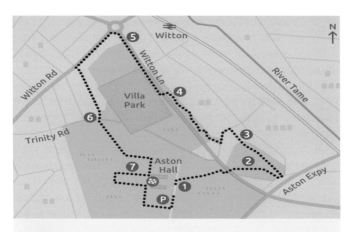

# AROUND ASTON HALL

*From Thomas Holte's mansion and park to a medieval village, church and tramway depot*

 Start/Finish: Front of Aston Hall, off Witton Lane. Postcode: B6 6JD.

 Bus: From City Centre stop at Aston Station.

 Parking: Aston Park.

 Facilities: Café at Aston Hall.

 Length: 2.5 km / 1.55 miles.
Mainly on pavements, also grass and unsurfaced paths in parks. Some steps.

 Dog-friendly.

 Time: 45 minutes.    Step count: 3,800 steps.

**START**

Aston Hall was built by Sir Thomas Holte between 1618 and 1635. It originally stood in a park which was much more extensive than the present-day Aston Park. Find out more by visiting Aston Hall Museum (birminghammuseums.org.uk)

**1** Walk down the main drive of Aston Hall and cross Witton Lane at the crossing to the church of St Peter and St Paul. Aston was a huge parish which extended to Deritend in the city centre and included Erdington, Castle Bromwich, Water Orton and Yardley. A priest at Aston is mentioned in Domesday Book in 1086 and his church was probably on this site. The church is first mentioned in about 1165, when it was given to Tickford Priory in Northamptonshire. The oldest part you can see now is the striking 15th-century tower. The rest of the church was completely rebuilt and considerably enlarged between 1879 and 1908 by the Birmingham architect J A Chatwin. Descriptions of the church before this show that it was mainly 13th- and 14th-century in date, but a blocked 12th-century doorway with a semi-circular head was exposed on the south side of the chancel during the 19th-century works. If the church is open, have a look at its magnificent cathedral-like interior. Its design

ASTON HALL

ASTON PARISH CHURCH FROM ASTON PARK

is thought to have been based on the old Coventry cathedral, which was severely damaged by bombing during the Second World War. Inside the church there are some medieval tomb effigies.

**2** Walk along the path past the porch heading towards the elevated motorway and exit the churchyard by a gap in the wall at the end of the path. Turn immediately to your left along a gravel path between the churchyard and Estone Drive. You are now walking through the site of medieval Aston! Directly to your left, Westbrook House, a timber-framed building of 15th- or 16th-century date stood on the edge of the churchyard, but was demolished in 1977. It may have been the priest's house. To your right is the spot where a map of 1758 shows a few houses, and archaeological excavations in 2013 on the site of the extension at the rear of Aston Tavern revealed drainage ditches and a sandstone wall.

The church and village stood alongside the river Tame. The hollow area in the woodland inside the churchyard, beyond the railings, is the original course of the river, which was diverted when the Grand Junction Railway was constructed in 1837.

**3** Follow the path until you come to Serpentine Road, named after the curving course of the river which originally turned to the north here. Turn left. The building on your left, now used as a mosque, is roughly on the site of a moat which is marked on a map of 1758 and may have surrounded the medieval manor house of Aston. At the junction with Holte Road turn left, then cross over the road and enter Witton Lane Gardens. This park is on the site of terraced houses demolished in the 1990s to make way for the rebuilding of the Witton Lane stand of Villa Park. The park around Aston Hall originally extended right up to Witton Lane. Villa Park was built in 1897 on the site of Dovehouse Pool, which provided ice for the 18th century icehouse at Aston Hall. Before this Aston Villa's ground was at Wellington Road in Handsworth.

**4** Leaving the park, continue along Witton Lane. On your right, beyond the car park, is the former Aston Manor tramway depot.

TRAM DEPOT

Its national importance was recognised by designation as a Listed building in 2012. It was built in 1882 for Aston Manor Borough Council; Aston did not become part of Birmingham until 1911. Steam-powered engines pulled the tram carriages and were housed in a lower building to the north of the main building. When trams were converted to run by electricity in 1904 they were double-decker, so the low building went out of use. A new roof was added to the taller building to accommodate tramcars and their overhead cables, and the frontage on Witton Lane was rebuilt at same time.

**5** At the junction locally known as Witton Island stands the Aston Hotel, dating to 1910. At the Island cross over the road and take the first exit, Witton Road. A little further along Witton Road the

Birmingham Settlement building opened in 1911 as the Pavilion Electric Theatre, where vaudeville acts performed and early movies were shown. Continue along Witton Road, which was the original boundary of the park around Aston Hall, and turn left into Nelson Road. This road with its terraced houses was built about 1900.

**6** Walk all the way down Nelson Road and enter Aston Park along a tree-lined path. This was part of the

LONDON PLANE TREES IN ASTON PARK

municipal landscaping of the park undertaken during the 1920s, making these London Plane trees nearly 100 years old. At the end of the path, turn to your left just before the steep flight of steps. The lower part of the unassuming brick structure you are approaching now was the basement of a 17th-century banqueting house which formed part of the formal gardens around Aston Hall. Take the small flight of steps up to the terrace above. Look through the railings towards the stable block and the excavated remains of the former north range. Walk around the edge of the terraced gardens and look down the hill. The park originally extended about twice as far as the distance to the present park boundary. As you return to the front of the hall, passing the formal gardens as you go, you can see the elevated Aston Expressway ahead. The park originally extended beyond the tower block in the distance and as far as Lichfield Road.

FINISH

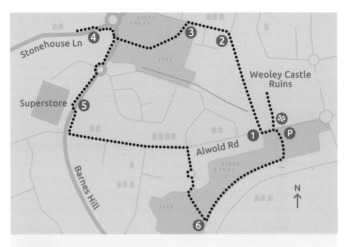

 **AROUND WEOLEY CASTLE**

*From a medieval manor house to a canal
and brickworks*

 Start/Finish: Weoley Castle ruins viewing area, off Alwold Road.
Postcode: B29 5RL.

 Bus service: From City Centre stop on Castle Road.

 Parking: On road opposite ruins.

 Facilities: Café at Barnes Hill superstore.

 Length: 2.75km / 1.71 miles.
On pavements, rough paths and across parkland. Some slopes.

 Dog-friendly.

 Time: 45 minutes.     Step count: 4,100 steps.

From Alwold Road, walk through the gates leading to the viewing area for the ruins. Interpretation panels tell you about the history of Weoley Castle. The Castle - which was really a fortified manor house - would have been surrounded by open land including a large deer park which extended as far as Selly Oak, Bristol Road and Shenley Lane. Find out more by visiting Weoley Castle (birminghammuseums.org.uk).

**1** Leaving Weoley Castle viewing area turn right and right again, taking a footpath that runs along the side of the site. After about 150m you will arrive at the brick parapet walls of a bridge over the line of what was the Dudley No 2 Canal. This was built in 1798 and ran from Dudley to the Worcester Canal at Selly Oak. It carried coal from the Black Country to brickworks around here - one of them was just to the left of the path.

RUINS OF WEOLEY CASTLE

**2** Continue up Somery Road (named after a family who owned Weoley Castle in the Middle Ages), a hollow way which would have been the original approach to Weoley Castle from the north, and turn left at the junction with Stonehouse Lane. To your left, look above the close boarded fence of the nursery. Through the trees you will catch a glimpse of Stonehouse Farm, which was probably built in the 17th century. Part of the building is brick and part is sandstone, probably taken from Weoley Castle. It is possible that Stonehouse Farm itself is medieval in origin and was a watchtower guarding the entrance to Weoley Castle. From Ullswater Close you can see the building's chimney stack.

**3** Further along Stonehouse Road, take the path on your left across Old Quarry Park and stop halfway across. This was the site of a brickworks. There were large pits where clay was dug to make the bricks, and the kilns in which they were fired. Isaac Flavell bought Stonehouse Farm in 1842 and established the brickworks. It was first known as California Brickworks, and later as Smart's, from its subsequent owner. Flavell is said to have emigrated to America and made a fortune in the California Gold Rush, which began in 1848. You are standing where the canal you saw earlier would have crossed the site, with a basin and wharfs serving the brickworks.

Looking down to your left across the open space, a line of trees marks the course of the Stonehouse Brook which fed water to the moat at Weoley Castle. From here cut across the grass to your right and cross the main road at the pedestrian crossing. Then walk up to the traffic island and turn left along Stonehouse Lane. The terraced houses here and the former Methodist Chapel a little further along the road were part of the settlement known as California, which developed in the 19th century. It was named after the nearby brickworks and was occupied by people who worked there. Bricks and tiles were being made in this area by the

PLAQUE

18th century, but the industry took place on a large scale from the 1840s and continued until the 1950s.

**4** Now retrace your steps back to the pedestrian crossing, noting the rough stone boundary walls on the side of the roads, probably made from material taken from Weoley Castle after it went out of use. Stop when you come to two large blocks of stone and a plaque set into the ground which commemorates the Lapal Canal Tunnel and the three brickworks of California. Another brickworks was established near here in the 19th century (the Superstore is on the site of the clay pit) and the large stones formed the base of a tramway that ran from the brickworks and under Barnes Hill to the canal basin in Old Quarry Park.

STONE QUARRY

**5** Continue along Barnes Hill past the Superstore and cross at the pedestrian crossing, then turn left into Alwold Road at the petrol station. After about 350 metres, turn right into Bilbrook Grove. At the end of the Grove take the path into the open space beyond and climb a steep hill. Within this parkland there was a quarry which was later used as a rifle range.

**6** Turn left at the top of the hill and walk along the mown path at the top of the slope until you reach a large tree. Enjoy the long views towards Birmingham City Centre and the Queen Elizabeth Hospital. From the tree, cross the path and make your way down the slope, walking across the grass until you reach an area of exposed red sandstone cut into the hillside. This was the stone used for Weoley Castle, and contrasts with the geology further west where the brickworks were using clay from mudstone. Take care whilst exploring the quarry remains then return to the entrance to Weoley Castle on Alwold Road.

FINISH

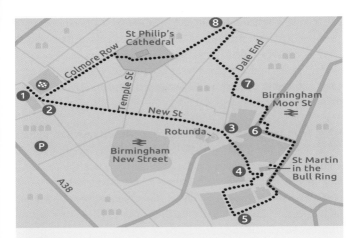

# MEDIEVAL BIRMINGHAM

 Start/Finish: Birmingham Museum & Art Gallery, Chamberlain Square. Postcode: B3 3DH.

 Bus service: Various services to and from City Centre stop nearby.

 Parking: Town Hall Car Park, Brunel Street, B1 1TA.

 Facilities: Café inside Birmingham Museum & Art Gallery.

 Length: 2.8 km / 1.74 miles.
Mainly on pavements. Some steps.

 Time: 50 minutes.  Step count: 4,200 steps.

Birmingham Museum & Art Gallery (BMAG) first opened in 1885. It is housed in a Grade II* listed city centre landmark building. There are over 40 galleries to explore that display art, applied art, social history, archaeology and ethnography. Find out more by visiting Birmingham Museum & Art Gallery (birminghammuseums.org.uk).

**1** From the BMAG main entrance turn left and walk into Victoria Square. This is the heart of Victorian Birmingham with its grand 19th century public buildings: BMAG, the Council House, the Town Hall and General Post Office. Pinfold Street opposite you (left of the old post office building) was part of the medieval road between Dudley and Birmingham, which continued through the site of New Street station then followed Dudley Street to Edgbaston Street. An old road surface was uncovered at the top of Pinfold Street during construction of the Metro line.

**2** Walk past the statue of Queen Victoria and bear left down New Street. Despite its name, this road was here in the 13th century.

BIRMINGHAM MUSEUM & ART GALLERY

It was probably built to create an improved road to Dudley, an important medieval town with a castle and priory. Continue along New Street with its 19th- and 20th-century buildings on either side. Just past the

54

EFFIGY IN ST MARTIN'S CHURCH

Temple Street crossroads you enter the medieval town where the road broadened out to form a market place. Continuing along New Street, look out for the blue plaque on the Trustee Savings Bank (TSB) marking the site of the medieval Guild Hall of the Holy Cross.

**3** At the bottom of New Street, bear to the right just past the Rotunda and take the central main route through the Bullring Shopping Centre. You will soon see the spire of St Martin's church ahead of you. Before taking the steps down to St Martin's pause at the statue of Lord Nelson, the first monument to be erected to the hero of Trafalgar in Britain. From here you have a good view of the heart of medieval Birmingham: the church with a market place in front of it where you are standing now the road leading downhill to cross the river Rea, Edgbaston Street to the right and the site of the medieval manor house beyond the church.

St Martin's church (open to visitors during the daytime, Monday to Saturday) was the parish church of medieval Birmingham. It was almost completely rebuilt in the 19th century but you can see some medieval walling inside the tower to the left as you enter the church and four stone effigies at the far east of the church that would have covered burials, probably of the lords of the manor of Birmingham, who named themselves after the town.

**4** Walk around to the right of St Martin's and then right along Edgbaston Street, past the famous Rag Market, then left into Gloucester Street. Excavations on the site of the Indoor Markets revealed remains of leather tanning from the 13th century onwards, using hides from cattle brought into the medieval market places. Turn left again onto Upper Dean Street. To your right was the medieval manor house. Excavations revealed the moat that surrounded it and a substantial stone wall of one of the 13th-century buildings.

**5** Continue along Upper Dean Street, past the outdoor market, and then turn left again approaching the east end of St Martin's. Just past the church walk back towards the shopping centre and look for an interpretation panel on your right (after about 20m) to find out more about the archaeological excavation of the churchyard. Then walk back the way you came and continue around the side of the Selfridges Building until you reach the turn in the road opposite Moor Street Station. Excavations before Selfridges and its car park (on the other side of Park Street) were built revealed a large 12th-century boundary ditch that divided the houses along the main road, opposite the church, from a deer park where the station now stands. Local clay was being used to make pottery here in the 13th century, and the potters dumped their waste pottery in the ditch.

**6** Cross three pedestrian crossings and head towards a modern brick building ahead of you, the church at Carrs Lane. Turn left here along Carrs Lane. Carry on to the junction with High Street, another medieval road which like New Street widened out to form a market place. Turn right, and at the next road junction you reach Dale End, the edge of the medieval town. The Welsh Cross stood here, and the Welsh

Market (both named after the origin of cattle brought here by drovers) occupied High Street between Carrs Lane and Dale End.

**7** Turn left along Bull Street, then right into Corporation Street, a 19th-century addition to the medieval town. Head towards the tower of the Central Hall but stop when you reach an open square (Priory Square) named after the medieval Priory or Hospital of St Thomas, a monastery which served travellers and the poor as well as the sick. The Priory was in existence by the 13th century and consisted of a chapel on Bull Street, a hall and other buildings. Look out for a mural and other public art in the square. Turn left taking a pedestrian route through the Minories. Some remains of the Priory were found here during building work in the 19th century. "Minories" refers to friars, but the Priory was actually occupied by Augustinian canons.

**8** When you reach Bull Street cross over into Temple Row and walk into St Philips's Cathedral Square. The cathedral was built in the early 18th century on open ground on what was then the edge of the town. Cross diagonally across the square until you reach Colmore Row, turn left and you will soon arrive back at Victoria Square.

FINISH

ST PHILIP'S CATHEDRAL

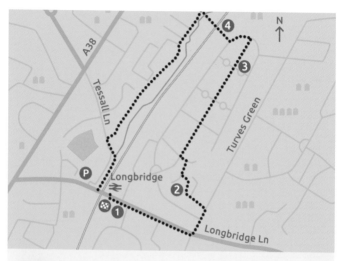

 ## LONGBRIDGE

*From Saxon settlers on the River Rea to a medieval moat and motor workers' houses*

 Start/Finish: Longbridge Station. Postcode: B31 2TW.

 Bus service: From City Centre stop at Longbridge Station.

 Parking: Longbridge Station.

Facilities: Many places in Longbridge Town Centre.

Length: 3km / 1.86 miles.
Mainly on pavements and surfaced paths.

 Dog-friendly.

 Time: 55 minutes.      Step count: 4,600 steps.

From the station, look to your right down the hill. The river Rea flows under the road near the station and then beneath Longbridge Town Centre, reappearing again in parkland near the shopping centre. Drainage channels dating to the 10th century AD were found under what is now the Innovation Centre (the modern brick building with green windows further up the hill to your right), together with pollen that shows that a thousand years ago the Rea Valley was partly wooded, with mainly alder and hazel trees, and there was grassland containing buttercups, dandelion and plantain. During the Middle Ages the trees were cleared for farming. Soil eroded by ploughing accumulated in the valley, and by the 16th century the landscape had changed to mainly open grassland.

**1** Cross at the pedestrian crossing then turn left and walk up Longbridge Lane. This is an ancient route leading to a crossing point of the Rea, and it was worn down into a hollow way through use

LONGBRIDGE LANE HOLLOWAY

MOATED SITE AT HAWKESLEY FARM

over hundreds of years. The raised grass bank on your left is a remnant of one side of the original hollow which survived the construction of the modern road. Turn left at the crossroads into Turves Green, at Longbridge Parish church, and then take the second left at Munslow Grove. Just before the block of flats there is an area of wet ground to your right surrounded by railings, the remains of the medieval Hawkesley Farm moat. To your left a garden fence, just before the first bungalow, dips into a hollow on the line of the 13th-century moat. Although it would have kept out unwanted visitors, the moat was constructed as a status symbol rather than for defence. Archaeological excavations before the bungalows and tower block were built showed that the moat surrounded a group of timber buildings constructed between the 13th and 15th centuries. An interpretation panel on the railing to your right describes the results of excavations and the siege of Hawkesley during the Civil War.

**2** Walk towards the group of bungalows ahead of you, where another interpretation panel shows how the main building on the site may have looked in the 15th century. This is based on architectural details of surviving medieval buildings such as the Saracen's Head in King's Norton. The seat behind you is built from stones found in the excavations. These would have been used for the footings for timber-framed walls, to raise them above the surrounding ground and prevent them from getting damp and rotting.

Take the path across the front of the bungalows until you come to another path with railings alongside it. From here you have a good view of the remains of the moat to either side. Take this path then turn right into Stokesay Grove. Walk past Bramber House on your left, then turn left along Walnut Way and right again into Central Avenue. You will soon come to a green sign welcoming you to The Austin Village.

AUSTIN VILLAGE

**3** Walk the full length of Central Avenue until you reach two blue plaques mounted on a brick plinth. The Austin Village was built in 1917 to house workers taken on by the Austin Motor Company to make tanks and aircraft for the war effort. In the space of four years the workforce multiplied tenfold, and since the factory was located in a rural area outside the city there was a need to accommodate workers as quickly as possible. The solution was to import 250 pre-fabricated cedar wood bungalows from Michigan in the USA. Because of the risk of fire, pairs of semi-detached brick houses were built at intervals as a precaution. The bungalows and houses were originally occupied as dormitories but were sold off as family homes after the war, when fewer workers were needed. Just beyond the blue plaques turn left into Hawkesley Crescent. Take the first footpath you come to on your right, between the houses, going downhill into the Rea Valley.

RIVER REA NEAR THE SITE OF HAWKESLEY / TESSALL MILL

**4** On your right just before the railway bridge was the site of Hawkesley or Tessall Mill, a corn mill which was in existence in the 13th century. There was a corn mill on this site until the later 19th-century, when many such mills ceased working because of competition from steam power.

Continue under the railway bridge (take care, because it is narrow here and there is no footpath), cross over the river on the footbridge and turn left along Rea Road. At the junction bear left then follow the cycle route signs until you come onto a path along the side of the river Rea. After 500 metres turn left onto Tessall Lane and then cross the bridge over the Rea. From here it is short walk back to Longbridge Station, which you will see on your left.

FINISH

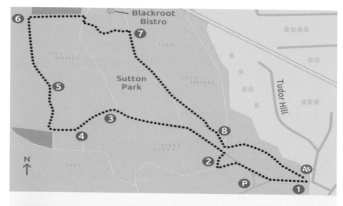

![boot icon] **SUTTON PARK- EAST**

*A medieval deer park, woods, mills and millpools*

 Start/Finish: Town Gate, Park Road. Postcode: B73 6BU.

 Bus service: From City Centre stop in The Parade.

 Parking: Town Gate entrance.

*Sutton Park is normally open all the time for pedestrian access. Gates for vehicular access to car parks are open by 9am all year but closing times vary in line with dusk and are indicated on gates.*

 Facilities: Café, Carvery and Bistro on route.

 Length: 3 km / 1.86 miles.
Mainly on tarmac roads and unsurfaced paths which may be muddy after rain. Some steps. Open water at park pools and streams.

 Dog-friendly.

 Time: 55 minutes.  Step count: 4,600 steps.

**START**

Sutton Park was created in the 12th century as a deer park. Later use of the Park included woodland management, animal grazing and military training as well as sport and recreation. The Park contains many well-preserved archaeological remains showing its different uses from prehistoric times onwards.

**1** Just inside Town Gate, next to the Town Gate Café, an interpretation panel tells you about the archaeology of Sutton Park. Walk alongside the road and at the fork in the road bear right, cross at the crossing and follow signs for the Carvery. Park House, now a pub and restaurant, is on the site of Blade Mill which was originally constructed in the 16th century. Most of the building you see now is 19th-century but the painted brick building on the left is part of the 18th-century watermill. There was a mill pool beyond fed by a stream called Ebrook or Plants Brook.

Before you reach the building, cross the bridge over a water channel into the car park on your right. Water flowed along this channel after turning the waterwheel by the mill back into the Brook. Cross the car park and

PARK HOUSE AND BLADE MILL

SITE OF MILL POOL

take a second bridge which crosses over the Brook itself into another car park then take an informal exit onto the road beyond (beware of traffic).

**2** Turn left along the road and continue past another car park and gate until you reach a narrow path to the left between two small stone pillars (one is fenced off), pause here. The marshy land beyond this is the site of the pool that powered Blade Mill. Returning to the road note the large hollow on the opposite side, one of several quarries dug in the past to extract the sand and pebbles underlying the Park. Continue along the road.

**3** Take a gravel path to the left leading to a crossing over the Brook. Here it has been straightened, and the small circular pool to your left was constructed in the 1930s. Along the stream to your right is a triple-arched brick bridge, one of four that were built across streams in

KEEPERS POOL

the park in the 19th century for the growing numbers of visitors.

**4** Follow the gravel path straight ahead until you reach the dam of Keepers Pool, originally constructed as a fishpond in the medieval deer park. Material to build the dam was dug out of the quarry to your right. Take the path up the hill to your right, and you can see more of the quarry, but beware of the steep drop into it!

**5** The path continues through the woods. This is Lower Nut Hurst, one of the ancient woodland areas of the park, which was managed as coppice from the 16th century onwards. Trees were cut down almost to their base and the shoots that grew up from them were cut at intervals and used for fuel and other purposes. Continue along the path. Just before you reach Blackroot Pool, a steep path runs up the hill to your left. Follow this for a short distance and on your right you will see a hollow in the ground. This is a saw pit, one of many in Lower Nut Hurst. Shoots cut from the coppiced trees would have been laid across the pit and sawn into smaller pieces by a man standing in the pit, so that they could be carried out of the woods more easily. The pit is on a slope and when the pit was made, the soil dug from it was piled onto one edge so that both sides were level.

Retrace your steps and continue towards Blackroot Pool. Just before you leave the wood you can see on your right part of its 16th-century boundary, consisting of some ancient hollies on a prominent bank with a ditch alongside. Topped with a fence, this boundary kept grazing animals out of the woods.

**6** Follow the path to your right along the dam. Blackroot Pool was constructed in 1757 by building a dam across the Ebrook or Plants Brook. It originally powered a mill that processed leather. At the end of the dam turn right and look for some concrete steps to your left which will take you up onto a path around the side of a former quarry, where

LOWER NUT HURST

CONCRETE STEPS

material to build the dam was dug out. Keep the wooden fence to your left until you reach an open space and Blackroot Bistro.

**7** Turn right on the main path ahead. As you continue along this path, on your left, you will see a triangular marker. This indicates a bank and ditch which was a subdivision of the medieval deer park. Continue along the path across a grassy area and you will see a marker which indicates another subdivision of the medieval deer park and the spectator banks of a 19th-century racecourse.

**8** You will see a car park down to your right. Do not walk towards it: instead take the path across the higher ground between the trees until you reach open ground beyond them. The 12th-century deer park originally extended right up to Sutton Coldfield town centre, which you can see in the distance from here, but it was later reduced in size. Take the path downhill and cross over the road into the field opposite then head for Town Gate in the far corner.

FINISH

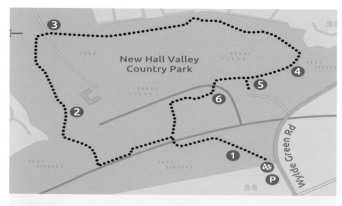

 **NEW HALL VALLEY**

*Waterworks for a mill, historic buildings and a burnt mound*

 Start/Finish: Car park on Wylde Green Road, Sutton Coldfield. Postcode: B72 1JB.

 Bus service: From City Centre stop on Birmingham Road.

 Parking: Wylde Green Road, Sutton Coldfield.

 Facilities: New Hall Hotel (advanced booking recommended).

 Length: 3 km / 1.86 miles.
On surfaced and grass paths and boardwalk. Can be muddy in wet weather.

 Dog-friendly.

 Time: 55 minutes.      Step count: 4,600 steps.

**START** From the car park take the main path into the Country Park. Soon after entering the park, you have views to your right towards a stone building, Vesey House (private, no public access). This was one of 51 cottages built in Sutton Coldfield in the 16th century by John Vesey, Bishop of Exeter, who was a native of the town and its great benefactor.

**1** Continue along the path until you cross a bridge over a stream and turn left. After about 250 metres take a boardwalk path through boggy ground to your right. At a viewing point on the right hand side you are crossing the headrace of New Hall Mill. Water was taken off the Ebrook further up the valley and along this channel to feed a mill pool. Continue along the boardwalk. At the end you'll come to a narrow winding path through reeds. Follow this path until you come to an area of woodland. Through the trees on your right you may catch glimpses of New Hall.

PATH BESIDE THE EBROOK

THE BOARDWALK

**2** Carry on uphill until you reach a green open space and bear right on the grassy path until you reach a permissive path which crosses the drive leading to New Hall. The oldest part of this moated house was built in the 13th century and extended and modernised during the 17th, 18th and 19th centuries. It was converted into a hotel in 1988. If you wish to visit the building it is possible book a table in the restaurant.

**3** Crossing into the field opposite, follow the grass path and gain more views of New Hall and its distinctive tower and cupola. You will soon reach a surfaced path which takes you past two children's play areas. Shortly after the second of these take a path to your right through woodland.

**4** When you reach the next junction cross over and through the gateway into the field opposite. A grass path runs downhill and in the distance to your left you will see a timber-framed building called Wincelle. It was built in the 17th century in Wiggins Hill and moved here in 1910.

**5** Continue downhill until you reach a gap in the hedge and cross this field until you reach another surfaced path. Before crossing the path walk downhill to your left a short distance and you will come to New Hall Mill, one of 10 watermills along the Ebrook. The buildings you can see now largely date from the 18th century but there has been a

FLIGHT OF WOODEN STEPS

watermill here since the 16th century, and some timber framing survives at the mill house. The mill is private but it is open to the public on set open days (check their website for more information).

Return back up the path to where you turned off and follow the path (now on your left) through the next field. Just past a picnic bench close to an access road for the mill take a flight of wooden steps ahead of you down to a bridge over the mill headrace. This fed the water to the mill pool which originally powered two water wheels and two pairs of millstones, grinding wheat to produce flour for the local area.

**6** Carry on downhill into the next field and where the path curves round to the left, just before you cross the brook, look out for a low grass-covered mound on the right surrounded by boggy ground. This is a burnt mound, composed of heat-shattered stones and charcoal dating to the Bronze Age, between about 1700 and 1000 BC. Burnt mounds have been interpreted as the debris from cooking in water brought to the boil by dropping heated stones into a trough. After several uses the stones eventually broke and were discarded to create the mound. An alternative interpretation is that they were the sites of sweat lodges or sauna baths where steam was produced by pouring water onto heated stones inside a tent-like structure. These sites are normally near a source of water and this burnt mound is near a former course of the Ebrook or Plants Brook.

**7** From here continue until you reach the main path through the Country Park. Follow this around to the left and it will eventually take you back to the car park.

FINISH

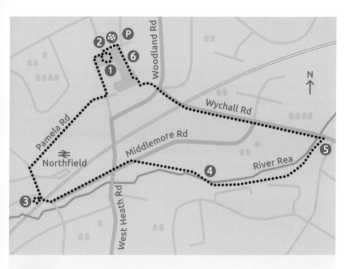

 # NORTHFIELD

## *From medieval buildings to industry and agriculture*

 Start/Finish: St Laurence church, Church Road. Postcode: B31 2LX.

 Bus service: From City Centre stop on nearby Bristol Road.

 Parking: Rectory Road.

 Facilities: Great Stone Inn.

 Length: 3.25km / 1.99 miles.
Mainly on pavements, some grass paths.
Open water along river Rea.

 Time: 1 hour 5 minutes.  Step count: 5,000 steps.

Enter the churchyard via the lych gate opposite the Great Stone Inn.

**1** Turn immediately left before the tower to see the north doorway. This is the oldest part of the church and dates to the 12th century. It was moved from its original position when the north aisle was built in the 19th century. The inner arch is carved with zigzags, and the outer is carved with `beak heads' with rounded eyes and pointed beaks, thought to represent the sin of the world. Carvings of animal heads on each side of the windows of the first floor of the tower are also 12th century. Go around the tower to the timber-framed 15th-century porch and inside you can see the pointed arch of the south doorway.

**2** Return to the lych gate, leave the churchyard and cross over Church Road. The 18th-century brickwork of the Great Stone Inn conceals a medieval timber-framed building, probably built in the 15th century. Its layout has been deduced from the surviving roof trusses. The central part, on each side of the present doorway, was a great hall which was open to the roof. Soot on the roof timbers shows that there was an open hearth

NORTHFIELD CHURCH, NORTH DOORWAY
WITH 'BEAK-HEADS'

VIEW DOWN CHURCH HILL

on the left hand side. The building probably originally extended over the site of the adjacent pound. The Pound dates to the 17th or 18th century and contains the Great Stone, a glacial erratic which formerly stood at the road junction near the corner of the pub and was moved here in 1954.

Walk back towards the church and take a right down Church Hill. Stop at the group of buildings on the corner. Watch out for oncoming traffic. These were built as two cottages and the darker-coloured over-fired bricks in the gable give a date of 1750, with the initials A W F. The chimney stack on the left includes a dovecote. The small single-storeyed building to the left of the cottages was probably a workshop where nails were made. It would have contained at least one hearth and an `oliver' (treadle-operated hammer). Nailmaking was an important local industry. A man called Naylor is mentioned in Northfield in 1594, and manual nailmaking continued here into the 19th century, when it was superseded by machine manufacture.

Looking up through the hedge to the left you can see the oldest part of St Laurence church of England Infant School, built in 1837, consisting of a two-storey master's house and a single-storey schoolroom. If you go along Norton Close to the right you can see the extension built in 1870.

Continue down Church Hill. The green open space here was the site of a farm until well into the 20th century. Turn right down Pamela Road then turn left into Quarry Lane and continue until you reach Mill Lane.

**3** Just before the railway bridge cross the road and take the footpath opposite. The interpretation panel tells you about Northfield Mill. Beyond the panel, next to the stone railway wall, you can see the brick wall alongside the mill pool dam and the brick footings of the water wheel pit.

Retrace your steps, leaving the mill site. Turn right, cross the road, walk under the railway bridge and then turn left into Station Road. The terraced houses here back onto the river Rea, and the modern group of houses opposite the station entrance are built on the site of a laundry. Cross West Heath Road and continue a short distance along Middlemore Road, turning right onto a path (Rea Valley cycle route) which takes you towards the river Rea.

**4** After about 250 metres cross a bridge over the river and take the path to your left. Keeping the river to your left, continue along the path and look out for lines of mature oak trees which run to your right and through the gardens of the nearby houses. These mark field boundaries which enclosed groups of former strips in a medieval open field.

**5** Stay on the path until you reach Wychall Road, leave the park and turn left. Continue until you cross the Birmingham and Gloucester Railway, which was built in 1840. Northfield Station opened in 1870. Cross Woodlands Road and take a footpath between the houses immediately opposite.

**6** Turn right at a junction in the paths, keeping the railing around the graveyard to your left. The modern houses to your right, just before you reach Rectory Road where the walk started, are built on the site of a moat which may have surrounded a medieval rectory.

FINISH

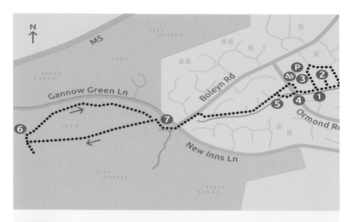

 **GANNOW GREEN**

*A medieval moat and fishponds on the river Rea*

 Start/Finish: Small car park off Ormond Road adjacent to the local store and community centre. Postcode: B45 0JD.

 Bus service: From City Centre stop on Ormond Road.

 Parking: off Ormond Road adjacent to the local store and community centre B45 0JD.

 Facilities: Café at Waseley Hills Country Park.

 Length: 3.2 km / 1.99 miles.
Mainly on pavements and footpaths, some across fields. Can be muddy after rain. The moat is water filled and the Rea is an open watercourse.

 Dog-friendly.

 Time: 1 hour 5 minutes.  Step count: 5,000 steps.

**START**

Take the footpath from the car park, just past the Lickey Banker Pub, marked Gannow Wood Walk. Beyond the fence on your right the river Rea flows in a cutting. Continue and stop just after crossing a bridge with metal railings.

**1** The boggy water-filled ditch of Gannow Green moat can be seen through the trees on your left. The moat surrounds a rectangular platform measuring approximately 40 metres x 60 metres, created by using the soil from digging the moat to build a slightly raised level surface on which to construct a house and other structures.

**2** Cross onto the moat platform along a raised causeway opposite a wooden fence a little further along the path. Excavations were undertaken in 1961 before the housing development around the site. Just over the causeway and to the right you can see a sunken rectangular area surrounded by a low bank where one of the digs took place. Archaeologists found a substantial sandstone wall on the inside edge of the moat dating from the 14th century. On the platform, there was evidence of timber-framed buildings with clay tiled roofs and a hearth, also constructed of clay tiles. This was a substantial medieval house; the stone wall was a status symbol rather than for defence.

Return to the path, continue to the corner and turn left at a litter bin onto another path along the eastern arm of the moat. At the end you come into Cornwall Road. Turn left and continue until you reach a turning area to your left.

**3** Cross the turning area and take a footpath bearing left, between bollards, to the rear of the shops. A narrow stream to your left originally kept the moat full of water. The site at the junction of the stream and the Rea was carefully selected for the moat, and the courses of the two watercourses were altered when the platform was constructed. When you reach the main path again, where the stream joins the river Rea under the bridge you crossed earlier, turn right back towards Ormond Road.

**4** Cross Ormond Road at the crossing and take a path into woodland left of the bus stop. Continue with the river on your right until you reach a bridge. Cross the bridge and on your right and ahead of you is a tree-covered embankment. This is the remains of a dam which formed a fish pond belonging to the moated site. The pond would have been to your left looking from the bridge where the river Rea flows, little more than a stream at this point, and would originally have covered Lismore Close. The southern bank of the pond can be seen clearly at the back of the houses in the distance showing that this was quite a large body of water. Fish were an important part of the medieval diet, and this tells us about the high status of the people who lived in the nearby moated house.

GANNOW GREEN MOAT

**5** Turn left along Lismore Close, keeping the river on your left, and continue on the footpath / cycleway along Skomer Close. Turn left when you reach Boleyn Road (look for blue Waseley Hills signs). Cross Gannow Green Lane and follow the footpath into the Country Park. After 150 metres turn left though a wooden kissing gate, striking uphill through a grassy field. Immediately on your left are lumps and bumps which are the remains of more medieval fishponds fed by the Rea. As you walk uphill you can see the remains of ridge and furrow, evidence that this area was farmed in medieval times. Pass through gaps in two hedges, and at the second head for the gate straight ahead of you.

**6** At the top gate turn left and you will shortly see a sign inside a fenced-off area which contains the source of the river Rea (it can be quite boggy, so take care). The Rea rises on the Waseley Hills (now in Worcestershire) and flows 15 miles north-east through Birmingham until it joins the river Tame just south of Spaghetti Junction. For much of its route is has been culverted, but it was very important in the development of Birmingham and its industries.

SOURCE OF THE RIVER REA

From here it is a short walk to the visitor centre for the Country Park where maps and refreshments are available. Walk uphill a short way and turn right along a path leading to a gate. You will see the carpark beyond.

Follow the tree-lined wooden fence that you passed through earlier. Carry on past the gate you came through and go through a wooden kissing gate between a group of holly bushes. You will come to a finger post; follow the route to Boleyn Road.

TREE LINED FENCE

**7** Retrace your steps when you get back to the main road. Walk down Boleyn Road, then Skomer Close. Instead of taking the bridge back over the Rea, continue along Lismore Close where it cuts through what was the dam of the fishpond. To your left, in a parking area off Mull Close, you can see a well preserved section of the dam. Continue to Ormond Road and cross back to the carpark.

FINISH

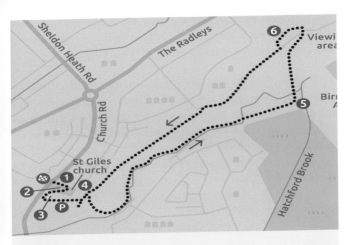

 ## SHELDON

### *From a rural past to roaring planes*

Start/Finish: St Giles church lych gate, Church Road, Sheldon.
Postcode: B26 3TT.

Bus service: From City Centre stop on Sheldon Heath Road.

Parking: at Sheldon Country Park off Ragley Drive (300m).

Facilities: Café at Rectory Farm.

Length: 3.7 km / 2.3 miles.
Mainly on surfaced footpaths and across grass. Westley Brook is
an open watercourse.

Dog-friendly.

Time: 1 hour 10 minutes.     Step count: 5,500 steps.

85

START

Before Sheldon became a residential suburb from the 1930s onwards, it consisted of scattered farms and houses with a small cluster of buildings around St Giles church.

**1** As you face the lych gate entrance to the churchyard, you can see a pair of Listed 18th-century cottages to your left. Walk along the drive between the churchyard wall and the cottages past the old school buildings which an inscription tells us were a 'Gift of Edward Earl of Digby 1852'. Just past the modern church hall turn right into the churchyard along a path through a gap in the brick wall and stop at the tower of St Giles church.

**2** There was a church here by the 13th century, but it was completely rebuilt in the 14th century. The tower was added in the 15th

SHELDON CHURCH

century: inscriptions inside tell us that it was built in 1461 and name the master mason as Henry Ulm. He was probably also responsible for towers in a similar style at other churches in the area, including Yardley and King's Norton. Continue along the path around the church. The timber-framed porch ahead of you was also built in the 15th century, and inside it you can see the door into the 14th-century nave. If the church is open, you can see the fine 14<sup>th</sup>-century timber roof. To the right of the porch, the 13<sup>th</sup>-century coffin lid carved with a cross was found in the churchyard in the 19th century, when the chancel and north aisle were rebuilt.

**3** Walk back through the churchyard towards the main road and take the path that forks to the left, passing through the churchyard then along a tree-lined path until you reach Ragley Drive. Over the road you can see a decorative Gothic-looking building which was constructed between the wars and is now used by the Royal Air Force Association, and a row of former farm cottages next to it. Go to the left along Ragley Drive. Just before the entrance to the main car park is the entrance to Rectory Farm, which you will see at the end of the walk.

**4** From the car park take the gate next to the playground and follow the finger-post sign towards Westley Brook. Take the path to the left before the brook (signposted Birmingham International Airport/ Marston Green). Follow this path alongside the brook, crossing two footbridges through woodland. A burnt mound was found on the stream bank near here. These mounds of heat-shattered stones and charcoal are the debris from cooking or steam bathing and tell us that people were living in this part of Birmingham 3000 years ago, in the Bronze Age. The houses they lived in were probably where the modern houses are now.

Carry on along the path crossing over a cycle route cutting across the park. Follow signs for Airport Viewing Area.

**5** After about 500 metres turn left along the path around the airport's perimeter fence. The viewing area is at the north end of the runway and laid out with benches. The path you have just walked along and the tarmac path it joins cross ridge and furrow, the remains of medieval cultivation. Depending on the wind direction this is a great place to watch aircraft landing and taking off. The airport was originally

PROMINENT RIDGE AND FURROW AT THE AIRPORT VIEWING AREA

built with a grass landing strip as Birmingham City Council's municipal airport. The first flights, to destinations in Great Britain only, took place in 1939. It was requisitioned at the outbreak of the Second World War and used for pilot training, aircraft flight testing and as a delivery base for bombers. Civilian flights resumed in 1946 and included European destinations from 1949. The terminal building and the runways were later extended to cater for increased passenger numbers and aircraft size.

**6** Go to the left along the tarmac path back through the country park. Where the path meets the cycle path crossing the park turn left, then strike right, across the grass, heading towards the tower of St Giles church which you can see in the distance. Return to the car park. If the gateway on the left is open make your way through to Old Rectory Farm. The Farm is a 17th-century timber-framed building encased in brick in the 18th century. It was the home of Thomas Bray who was rector of

RECTORY FARM – NOW A CAFÉ AND URBAN FARM AT SHELDON COUNTRY PARK

St Giles church from 1690. Look for a blue plaque commemorating him on the front of the house. Old Rectory Farm replaced an earlier building of medieval date surrounded by a moat, which was in the field to the rear of the tea room patio area behind the farmhouse. The stables, pigsties and other outbuildings now accommodate a children's farm.

FINISH

 **SUTTON PARK – WEST**

*From a medieval deer park to a Roman road and Victorian soldiers*

 Start/Finish: Banners Gate, Monmouth Drive. Postcode: B73 6JX.

 Bus service: From City Centre stop at Kingstanding Circle approx. 1km from Banners Gate.

 Parking: Banners Gate entrance.

*Sutton Park is normally open all the time for pedestrian access. Gates for vehicular access to car parks are open by 9am all year but closing times vary in line with dusk and are indicated on gates.*

 Facilities: Refreshments kiosk next to Banners Gate playground.

 Length: 4 km / 2.49 miles.
Mainly on surfaced and unsurfaced paths. May be muddy after rain.

 Dog-friendly.

 Time: 1 hour 5 minutes.  Step count: 5,800 steps.

**START**

Sutton Park was created in the 12th century as a deer park. Later use of the park included woodland management, animal grazing and military training as well as sport and recreation. The Park contains many well preserved archaeological remains showing its different uses from prehistoric times onwards.

**1** Start the walk just before the entrance to the park. Banners Gate Lodge to the left of the entrance was built in 1855 when public use of the park was increasing. It was occupied by a tenant who watched the gate and was employed as a "woodman, hedge carpenter, etc." From the entrance walk into the park and take the first path into the woods on your left, just past the lodge. Continue along a woodland path just inside the park boundary, which follows the boundary of the 12th-century deer park. Looking through the trees towards the road, between the path and the fence, you will see the ditch and bank which were built in the 12th century to prevent deer escaping from the park. With a fence on top of the bank, they formed a barrier which was too high and too wide for deer to jump over.

A little further along the path, look out for a group of mature chestnut trees. Beneath one of these is a hollow in the ground just to the left of the path. This is a saw pit. Large branches cut from the trees would have been laid across the pit and sawn into smaller pieces by a man standing in the pit, so that they could be carried out of the woods more easily.

**2** Continuing along the path, with the road on your left, you will come to a clearing with more mature chestnut trees. Take the path slightly to your right. This soon goes over a raised bank with a ditch alongside it which was constructed in the 18th century around Westwood Coppice, the woodland you have just walked through. With a fence on top of the bank, this boundary kept out grazing animals who would eat the young shoots that grew from the bases of cut trees in the coppice. Take the straight path through the woods ahead of you until

CLEARING

you come to a cinder track, and turn right along it. This is Lord Donegal's Ride, a route created in the 18th century by the Earl of Donegall (who lived at Fisherwick near Lichfield) as a route for fox hunters riding into the Park.

**3** On the left of the track you will see a low triangular marker which indicates the location of a Roman road, known as the Ryknield or Icknield Street, built in the 1st century AD between forts at Wall near Lichfield and Metchley near Edgbaston. Walk to the left along the bank of the road for a short distance. On its surface you can see the gravel it is made of and beneath the trees to the left, a short distance from the road, you can pick out shallow hollows where the gravel was dug for its construction. To each side of the road and running parallel to it there are slight narrow ditches which were dug by military surveyors to mark out the line of the road and indicate the area where vegetation had to be cleared to build it.

ROMAN ROAD

CONCRETE LINED TRENCH

**4** Return to Lord Donegal's Ride and continue for about 400 metres heading for a group of pine trees in the distance. Under the trees you can see a concrete-lined trench that sheltered soldiers who manned the targets of a 19th-century rifle range. The targets were just behind the trench, and soldiers fired at them from points at various distances on the range, which ran alongside Westwood Coppice. The mound behind the

PATH THROUGH HEATHLAND

trenches caught stray shot. Now return the way you came for a short distance and take the first clear rough path to your left across an area of heathland. Just after you cross a drainage ditch with large pebbles exposed, follow a clear grass path heading right towards woodland and you will soon arrive at a wide gravel path.

**5** Turn left onto this path which leads you back to the car park at Banners Gate. To the right of this path you will see a bank and ditch which form the boundary of Westwood Coppice. This woodland is set apart from the rest of the park's ancient woodland, which is on the eastern side of the park. It is straight-sided and rectangular in contrast to the curving shapes of the other woods because it was newly planted in the 18th century. Acorns were probably planted in 1776, when Westwood Coppice was ploughed, and a crop of corn was sown and subsequently harvested. The oak seedlings would be protected by the faster-growing corn, which could be harvested by hand without damaging the seedlings.

Oaks were planted for timber and sweet chestnuts for coppicing across an area covering 47 acres. However, the woodland was not managed for long, perhaps because it was no longer profitable as coal and coke became more popular fuels for industry and domestic use.

Continue along the path to return to the Banners Gate car park. An interpretation panel here tells you more about the archaeology of Sutton Park and gives information about other walking trails created by the Friends of Sutton Park.

FINISH

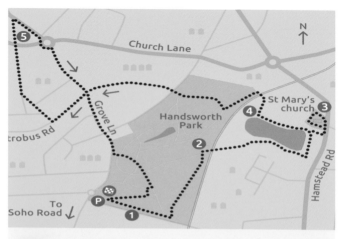

 **HANDSWORTH**

*From a Victorian park to medieval buildings*

 Start/Finish: Handsworth Park. Postcode: B20 2BY.

 Bus service: From City Centre stop on Grove Lane.

 Parking: Wellbeing Centre.

 Facilities: Many places on Soho Road.

 Length: 4.25 km / 2.64 miles.
On pavements and paths in park. Alongside open water near pool in the park. Some steps leading to the church.

 Dog-friendly.

 Time: 1 hour 15 minutes.  Step count: 6,100 steps.

**START** Handsworth Park was opened in 1888. Formerly known as Victoria Park, it was created from pleasure grounds and meadows around The Grove, an 18th-century villa which was later known as Park House. Its site is now occupied by the Wellbeing Centre. The park was subsequently enlarged to include land on the other side of the railway.

**1** From the car park make your way along the Broad Walk to the Holly Road entrance to the park. To your left you will see two tree-lined paths. Take the path bearing to the right.

You will soon reach a bridge on your right which crosses the railway line. Before crossing, look at the bandstand a short distance away to your left. The structure dates to 1891, but it was moved to this location in 1907 and restored in 2000. Musical concerts were very popular in public parks up until the outbreak of the Second World War, after which many fell into decline or were demolished. This fine example is a rare survival in the

HANDSWORTH PARK – GENERAL VIEW

BANDSTAND

City. The railway opened in 1889 and closed in 1941. It was constructed by the LNWR between their New Street to Wolverhampton and New Street to Walsall lines, particularly to serve goods traffic, including the coal mine at Hamstead.

**2** At the other side of the railway bridge take the path along the side of the lake. This was created in 1897 as a boating pool, replacing two long narrow ponds which may have been constructed as fishponds in the Middle Ages. Continue along the path to a lodge with a clock tower. This was built in 1897 close to the former church rectory, which may have been built on the site of a medieval manor house surrounded by a moat extending from one of the narrow ponds. Alternatively, another moat just over the road from the church may have surrounded the manor house. In 1272 John Eleford drowned when he fell off the drawbridge into the moat around the manor house, then owned by William de Parles.

When you reach the end of the path, just before the park entrance, turn left, passing a cast iron canopy (umbrello) that once covered a drinking fountain, then take the next exit from the park on your right, turn left and enter the churchyard.

**3** St Mary's church is medieval in origin, but it was almost wholly rebuilt and enlarged in the 19th century, mainly by the Birmingham architect J A Chatwin between 1876 and 1880. The oldest part of the church you can see now is the tower, which was constructed in the 12th century and heightened in the 15th century. On the other side of the church, the Wyrley chapel with its two triple windows was built in the 16th century. If you go inside the church you can see a filled-in 12th century window on the wall of the tower and two 16th century

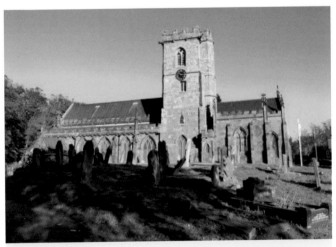

ST MARY'S CHURCH

monuments. The pioneering industrialists Matthew Boulton, James Watt and William Murdoch (mispronounced Murdock by his English colleagues) are buried here. Boulton and Murdoch are commemorated by memorials with their busts and there is a statue of Watt in the chapel bearing his name. In the churchyard look out for a modern memorial to gypsies who were buried in here between 1889 and 1915.

Return to the park and take the path alongside the lake, keeping the churchyard on your right. There was a long narrow pond between the path and the churchyard before the lake was constructed in the 19th century.

S S JOURNEY

**4** When you reach a piece of sculpture, the SS Journey (inspired by the migration to Handsworth of people from all over the world from the 1940s onward), turn right then left taking a footbridge crossing the railway. Take the path to the right around the edge of the cricket ground and leave the park at Hinstock Road, crossing into Philip Victor Road. At Grove Lane cross into Antrobus Road and then take a footpath on your right next to no 52. Continue straight on until you reach Laurel Road. Turn right, continue along Laurel Road, passing Laurel Road Community Centre on your left. Then cross at the junction with Oxhill Road into Slack Lane opposite, and continue for about 100 metres.

**5** The timber-framed building on your right, just before the junction with College Road, is the Old Town Hall, named because it was in the "Town End" hamlet of Handsworth. The panels between the timbers in the walls would originally have been filled with wattle and daub but this was replaced by bricks in the 17th century. At the end of the building you can see two curving timbers or crucks supporting the roof and walls. We do not know the exact date of this building, but tree-ring dating of other cruck-framed buildings in the Birmingham area shows that they were built in the 15th century. There is a small museum inside the building run by the Handsworth Historical Society (check their website for opening times).

Turn right on College Road then cross at the roundabout into Grove Lane. After about 500 metres on your left the former Grove Lane Baths (now converted to flats) were built on the site of Grove Farm and opened in 1907. They provided First and Second Class Swimming Baths, suites of First and Second Class Private Baths for Men and Women and Turkish Baths designed in an Eastern style. Re-enter Handsworth Park and take the path that bears to the right, passing the Sons of Rest Building, which was built in 1937 to replace a timber structure. Return around to the Wellbeing Centre.

FINISH

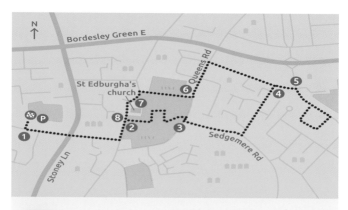

 **AROUND BLAKESLEY HALL**

*Before Blakesley- medieval Yardley*

 Start/Finish: Blakesley Hall, Blakesley Road. Postcode: B25 8RN.

 Bus service: City Centre stop in Bordesley Green East.

 Parking: Blakesley Hall or on street nearby.

 Facilities: Café at Blakesley Hall.

 Length: 4.25 km / 2.64 miles.
Mainly on pavements, with some paths and grass in park.

 Dog-friendly.

 Time: 1 hour 15 minutes.  Step count: 6,100 steps.

**START**

Tree-ring dating of its timbers shows that Blakesley Hall was built in 1590, but it also contains some timbers recycled from an earlier building on the site. Excavations under the service range, to the right of the porch, revealed a pebble surface containing 13th-century pottery and a geophysical survey to the north of the building located a probable moat. Find out more by visiting Blakesley Hall Museum (birminghammuseums.org.uk)

**1** Leaving the entrance of Blakesley Hall turn left along Blakesley Road, cross at the crossing over Stoney Lane and continue straight on along Blakesley Road until you reach Church Road then turn left. Ahead you will see the spire of St Edburgha's church. Before you reach the church building, stop at the timber-framed old Grammar School (Trust School). This was built in the 15th century and consists of a large room on each floor. Look at the detail of the carvings on the timbers, particularly at the corners. The schoolmaster recorded in Yardley in 1402, before this building was constructed, probably taught in the church.

ST EDBURGHA'S CHURCH AND THE OLD GRAMMAR SCHOOL

RIDGE AND FURROW IN OLD YARDLEY PARK

**2** Retrace your steps a short distance and take a left through the rose garden into Old Yardley Park. In a short while you will see a group of trees on your left, opposite the playground. Just inside the trees you can pick out a wide shallow ditch, the remains of a medieval earthwork known as Rents Moat. The de Limesi family lived at Rents Moat during the 13th century and they may have been responsible for constructing the church. The original timber-framed house that once stood here was demolished in about 1700 when the family moved away. The water-filled moat remained but was infilled for safety reasons in 1900, when the Yardley Great Trust gave land between Church Road and Queens Road to create Old Yardley Park. Walk around the edge of the trees, looking out for the line of the moat, until you return to the path you started on, and carry on through the park. On each side of the path you can see ridge and furrow, the remnants of a medieval open field system where each person farmed several strips of land scattered through the field.

**3** Leave the park, cross the road at the crossing and walk along Sedgemere Road. Then take the first left along Partridge Road. These roads follow old field boundaries. The houses on the left were constructed between the two world wars, when Yardley was becoming a suburb of Birmingham.

**4** At Broadstone Road turn right, then right again into Sheldon Heath Road and then right once more into the Hayes Kents Moat. As you walk along the road you can see the moat on your left. It was originally 9 metres wide and 3 metres deep, and filled with water. Before the modern houses (private property, no access) surrounded by the moat were built archaeologists uncovered remains of timber-framed medieval buildings dating from the 12th to 14th centuries, including a great hall, solar and kitchen. Some of the buildings had decorated floor tiles and some windows had coloured glass. Continue walking around the moat until you are back on Sheldon Heath Road. Take a left when you reach this road. On your left you will soon see the access road to the modern houses on the platform. This is where the original bridge over the moat would have been.

KENTS MOAT

**5** Return to Broadstone Road, which together with Pool Way opposite is on the line of a road called 'the way of the Dagard folk', mentioned as a point on the boundary of Yardley in an Anglo-Saxon charter of AD 972. Turn left along Broadstone Road, and continue until you reach the Queens Road junction. Cross over the road and turn left onto Queens Road.

**6** In about 200 metres a path on the right will take you along the edge of Old Yardley Park. The footpath leads to School Road, where the Victorian village school, now the church hall, stands on the corner. Turn left along Church Road into the village. To your right is a group of farm buildings set around a yard, dating from the 18th and 19th centuries; reminders that until well into the 20th century Yardley was a village surrounded by fields in a rural setting.

**7** Go up steps onto the grass in the churchyard and look at this side of the church. There was a chapel here by 1165 but the oldest parts you can see now date from the 13th century. Unlike most of the other medieval churches in Birmingham it was not substantially rebuilt by the Victorians. The tower was built in the 15th century in a similar style to other local church towers, including Sheldon and King's Norton. They may have been built by the same master mason, Henry Ulm. Above the doorway in the wall to the left of the tower are carved a Tudor rose and a pomegranate. These are the symbols of Katharine of Aragon, and may relate to the fact that Yardley manor was given to her on her divorce from Henry VIII. Walk to the left around the east end of the church to the other side and tucked behind the boiler house you can see the oldest surviving part of the church - a narrow pointed 13th-century window with a small doorway under it. Continuing around the church you reach the porch, built of substantial oak timbers and dating to the 15th century. Inside it you can see a 13th century doorway. Look out for grooves at the base of the tower, where arrows, swords, knives, scythes or sickles have been sharpened.

Retrace your steps back to Blakesley Hall. Pass Old Yardley Park on your left before taking a right down Blakesley Road. Follow this road all the way back to Blakesley Hall.

FINISH

BLAKESLEY HALL

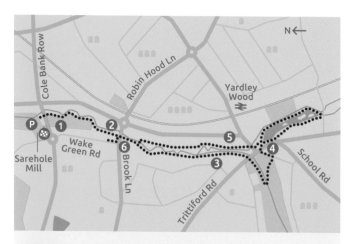

 **AROUND SAREHOLE MILL**

*Exploring the waters of the River Cole and its streams*

 Start/Finish: Sarehole Mill, Cole Bank Road. Postcode: B13 0BD.

 Bus service: From City Centre stop on Cole Bank Road.

 Parking: Car Park for Sarehole Mill on Cole Bank Road.

 Facilities: Café at Sarehole Mill.

 Length: 5km / 3.11 miles.
On pavements, surfaced paths and grass alongside open water.

 Dog-friendly.

 Time: 1 hour 30 minutes.    Step count: 7,500 steps.

108

**START**

You are standing at the entrance to Sarehole Mill. There was a mill on the site of Sarehole Mill in the 16th century but the oldest surviving parts are 18th century in date. There used to be a total of 13 watermills on the river Cole and its tributaries in Birmingham. Find out more by visiting Sarehole Mill Museum (birminghammuseums.org.uk).

**1** From Sarehole Mill car park cross over Cole Bank Road at the crossing, go through the gate into a wooded area, and follow the John Morris Jones Walkway, part of the Shire Country Park. The ditch next to the fence on entering the woodland was a spillway. It carried water from the headrace that fed Sarehole Mill to the river Cole when water was high, preventing it flooding a field where cattle grazed. After a short walk along the riverside path you will come to a grassy field on the right. The headrace feeding Sarehole Mill Pool was on the other side of this field, running along the back of the houses you can see in the distance.

**2** Continue on the path along the river to Brook Lane, cross over the road at the crossing, and then go down Coleside Avenue. You will pass a brick arched bridge to your left but carry on along the road and take the path signposted the Dingles. The ditch on the left of the path just after the gate is the headrace of Sarehole Mill. A little further along you will see a concrete bridge to your left, crossing the headrace which branches off the main river

RIVER COLE

CHINN BROOK

course near here. Stay on the reinforced path until you reach another narrow bridge to your left (near a signpost) which crosses the tailrace of the next mill along the valley at Trittiford. If you stop and look from this bridge you can see the junction of the tailrace and river.

**3** Continue on the path until you reach Trittiford Road, cross over and follow the path to the left of the children's playground, signposted Cocks Moor Woods Nature Reserve. The stream to your left is the Chinn Brook. It originally flowed directly into the river Cole but was diverted into the tailrace for Trittiford Mill when the mill was built. Walk along the path and cross the brook by the bridge on the left signposted Trittiford Mill Pool. Along Chinn Brook to your right were two prehistoric burnt mounds. These mounds of heat-shattered stones and charcoal are the debris from cooking or steam bathing and tell us that people

TRITTIFORD MILL POOL

were living in this part of Birmingham 3000 years ago. The houses they lived in were probably where the modern houses are now. Once you have crossed the bridge bear left and go uphill along a path across open grassland. Where the path curves to the right, a slight hollow runs up to a clump of willow trees on your left. This is the remains of a headrace for Trittiford Mill, taking water from further up the Chinn Brook to a pool next to the mill.

**4** Walk past a small car park and turn left down Highfield Road. The headrace flowed into a small pool that served Trittiford Mill. The mill, which was in existence by 1779, stood near the modern houses on the opposite side of the road. Continue to the junction, cross over Priory Road, and enter Trittiford Mill Park. Take the path to the left going around the mill pool. To your left you see glimpses of the river Cole below through the trees. You are now walking along the dam that was constructed to hold the water in the pool, which covers about 8 acres. At the far end the pool narrows and you cross a bridge over the headrace which takes water from the river Cole to feed the pool. Then turn right and walk back along the other side of the pool. Leave the park where you entered.

At the traffic island bear right and cross over Highfield Road. Then cross the road bridge over the river.

**5** At the end of the bridge, turn left into parkland and walk along a mown grass path, with the river Cole to your left. After about 500 metres you reach an area of open grassland where you can see ridges running across the grass at right angles to the river. These may be remains of medieval ploughing or water meadows, in which water flowed along the ridges from the river when it overflowed, depositing fertile silt onto the land.

A little further along the path look out to your left for a footbridge over the river. From this bridge the headrace for Sarehole Mill left the river at the end of the brickwork you can see on the far bank. Return to the path and continue with the river on your left. The path narrows and eventually you will cross the river by the brick arched bridge you saw earlier. Cross this bridge, then turn right along John Morris Jones Walkway back into Coleside Avenue.

PREFABS IN WAKE GREEN ROAD

**6** Cross over Brook Lane at the crossing and go to your left into Wake Green Road. The prefab houses here were built in 1945. This type of temporary accommodation was built for people who had lost their homes through bombing during the Second World War. Many prefabs were built in Birmingham, often on the edges of parks, but very few survive. These prefabs are now protected as Listed Buildings. Return to Brook Lane and turn left. Turn left again, retracing your steps along John Morris Jones Walkway.

You will soon arrive back at Cole Bank Road. Cross over the road at the crossing and you are back at the entrance to Sarehole Mill, cared for by Birmingham Museums. If you visit the mill you can see the machinery inside it and the adjoining mill pool.    FINISH

SAREHOLE MILL

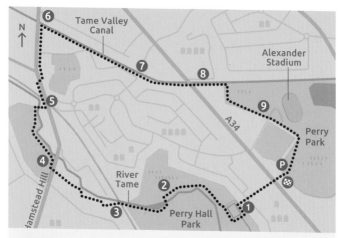

 ## PERRY AND HAMSTEAD

*From a medieval moat to a railway, canal and coal mine.*

Start/Finish: Walsall Road, at junction with Perry Avenue and Church Road. Postcode: B42 1TZ.

Bus service: From City Centre stop on Walsall Road.

Parking: Car park for Perry Park, at the junction of Walsall Road and Church Road.

Length: 5.4km / 3.36 miles.
Mainly on surfaced paths, also grass and unsurfaced paths in parks and pavements. Hilly in places, alongside open water in places, with some steep steps.

Dog-friendly.

Time: 1 hour 35 minutes.  Step count: 8,000 steps.

**START**

Walk from Walsall Road along Perry Avenue.

**1** Just inside Perry Hall Park you can see the moat that once surrounded Perry Hall. The rectangular moat was filled by water carried along a channel from the nearby river Tame. Perry Hall was a large house built of brick in 1576. It replaced an even older timber-framed building. Many manor houses and other buildings in the Birmingham area between the 12th

PERRY HALL MOAT

and 14th centuries had moats. They would have kept out unwanted visitors, but were more of a status symbol than for serious defence. Perry Hall was demolished in 1931 and the site was laid out as the formal gardens you see today.

Take the path to the left around the outside of the moat and to your left you will come to a hollow with a stream running through it that was originally a fishpond. It may have once been the original course of the river Tame. Continue round the edge of the moat and stop at the corner near the outdoor gym. In the grass between the path and the river you may be able to see slight ridges and furrows, the remains of cultivation dating back to medieval times.

Continue to your right around the moat and past the 1930s concrete bridge that crosses it. Bear left along a road that goes past a car park. The river Tame is to your left here, behind a low embankment built to prevent it from overflowing into the parkland. Leave the gravel path where the river turns to your left and follow the path alongside the river. Head for a bridge in the distance and stop and look across towards the edge of the park. Beyond the trees is the site of Perry Barr colliery. A shaft was sunk here in 1875 to mine coal from the same seam as Hamstead Colliery, but it soon went out of use.

**2** Cross over the river and take the path to the right, alongside the river. You are now on the River Tame Way.

**3** After about 300 metres the path passes under a modern bridge. It carries a railway line that was opened in 1837 as part of the Grand Junction Railway. This was one of the first railway lines to be built in England, and arguably the world's first long-distance railway. You can see the lower part of the original stone railway bridge over the river Tame, and rubble from the demolished sections in the river bank. Continue along the path through parkland until you reach a main road (Old Walsall Road) and cross at the crossing.

**4** On the other side of the road, near the children's playground, you will find an 18th century road bridge over the river. This was once the main road between Walsall and Birmingham. Continue on the path alongside the river. To your left, on the playing fields just past the pavilion, is the site of Hamstead Mill which may have been in existence at the time when the Domesday Book was written in the 11th century. Its mill pool would have extended to the other end of the playing fields. Continue along the river until you reach a late 18th- or early 19th-century brick bridge over the river Tame.

**5** Cross the bridge and walk towards Hamstead Station. Turn left along Old Walsall Road then cross the road by the shops and continue along it, looking out on your left for a memorial to the 26 miners who lost their lives in the 1908 Hamstead Colliery disaster. At one time the Colliery, which was in operation from 1875 to 1965, had the deepest seam in the world at nearly 2000 feet. Continuing uphill, in the distance you will see the aqueduct that carries the Tame Valley

Canal over the main road. Looking to your right into Kingsdown Avenue you will see a green open space, the site of Hamstead Brickworks which closed in the 1960s. Carry on uphill towards the aqueduct and just before you get there look for some steep steps, next to a gas sub-station, leading up to the canal towpath.

**6** Walk up the steps to the Tame Valley Canal, built by Act of Parliament in 1839 and opened in 1844. Turn right and walk along the towpath. This was a huge engineering feat, built to tackle congestion on the canals in the city centre at a time when the railways were setting up in competition. The canal is 13.5 km long and joined the Walsall Canal to the Birmingham and Fazeley Canal at Salford Junction near Spaghetti Junction. The canal is wide and straight and had towpaths on both sides. At first you are walking along an embankment, but you are soon level with the surrounding area. After the Marine Youth Group site you enter a deep cutting blasted out of the rock to either side. The waste from here was used to create the level embankment you have walked along.

FREETH BRIDGE OVER TAME VALLEY CANAL

**7** Look closely at the geology on either side, which was laid down around 300 million years ago and includes layers of red sandstone and pebbles. You can see the chisel marks where the sides of the cutting were finished off by the workers who built the canal. Passing beneath the 19th century Freeth Bridge, the cutting becomes less deep as you approach the 1930s road bridge that carries the Walsall Road across the canal.

CANALSIDE BUILDINGS

**8** Walk under the bridge and look at the canalside buildings dating from the 1840s including old stables, a gauging weir house and lock-keepers cottage and office. This is the start of a flight of 13 locks taking the canal down 30 metres to the Salford Junction. Walk past the first two locks, heading towards the cast iron footbridge, go under the bridge and here leave the canal taking the path to the right.

**9** From here you will see the home of the 2022 Commonwealth Games at the Alexander Stadium on your left. Follow the path around the site. The brick buildings in the distance to the right are those of the Birmingham Crematorium constructed in 1903, one of the earliest such facilities in the country to be built following the Cremation Act of 1902.

Continue walking through the car park and past the stadium and eventually you will arrive at Perry Park. Turn right and cross the green space, following the route of the access road and heading back to the car park and Walsall Road.

FINISH

# FINDING OUT MORE

**All of Birmingham:**

M. Hodder, Birmingham: *The Hidden History* (Tempus, 2004/ The History Press, 2011)

A. Foster, *Birmingham* (Pevsner Architectural Guides, Yale, 2005)

P. Leather, *A Guide To the Buildings of Birmingham* (Tempus, 2002)

W. Dargue, A History of Birmingham Places and Place Names A to Y, https://billdargue.jimdo.com/

Birmingham City Council, *Historic Environment Record* https://localview.birmingham.gov.uk/Planning/Sites/her/

Birmingham City Council, *Historic Landscape Characterisation* https://www.birmingham.gov.uk/info/20056/archaeology/50/historic_landscape_characterisation/2

**Individual walks:**

**Around Aston Hall:** O. Fairclough, *The Grand Old Mansion: The Holtes and Their Successors at Aston Hall, 1618-1864* (Birmingham Museum & Art Gallery, 1984)

**Around Blakesley Hall:** V. Skipp, *Medieval Yardley* (Phillimore, 1970)

**Harborne:** E. Chitham, *Harborne: A History* (Phillimore, 2008)

**King's Norton:** G. Demidowicz and S. Price, *King's Norton: A History*, (Phillimore, 2009)

**Around Sarehole Mill:** J. M. Jones, *The Cole Valley South (The Millstream Way)* (River Cole and Chinn Brook Conservation Group, 1989)

**Sheldon:** V. Skipp, *Discovering Sheldon: A Brief History of a Birmingham Parish from Anglo-Saxon to Modern Times* (University of Birmingham, 1960)

**Around Soho House:** S. Mason, *Matthew Boulton: Selling What All The World Desires* (Yale, 2009)

**Sutton Coldfield Centre and New Hall Valley:** R. Lea, *The Story of Sutton Coldfield* (Sutton, 2003)

**Sutton Park - West and East:** M. Hodder, *The Archaeology of Sutton Park* (The History Press, 2013)

# ACKNOWLEDGEMENTS

This book was developed by M. Hodder and S. Whitehouse and the team at Birmingham Museums Trust.

Maps illustrated by Tom Woolley.

Photographs supplied by M. Hodder, S. Whitehouse, V. Milligan and A. Nicholson-Evans.

All other images copyright Birmingham Museums Trust.

# GLOSSARY

*A small selection of terms that appear on several of the walks.*

*Burnt mound:* a mound of heat-shattered stones and charcoal, usually near a stream, dating from 1500-1000 BC. Hot stones were used to boil water for cooking or to create steam for sauna bathing.

*Headrace and tailrace:* artificial channels constructed to take water off a river upstream from a mill, increasing the height of water to drive the waterwheel (the headrace) and to return water back to the river level (the tailrace).

*Medieval/Middle Ages:* period from the Norman Conquest (1066) to the middle of the 16th century.

*Moated site:* a ditch, usually originally water-filled, surrounding a house and other buildings, built between the 12th and the 14th centuries as a status symbol rather than for defence.

*Ridge and furrow:* remains of fields where the soil was ploughed into ridges to improve drainage. The ridges formed strips in a medieval open field, and each person farmed several strips scattered through the field.

# NOTES